CW00420992

Grandma Gatewood:
Ohio's Legendary Hiker
By: Kelly Boyer Sagert
and Bette Lou Higgins

Grandma Gatewood: Ohio's Legendary Hiker

By: Kelly Boyer Sagert and Bette Lou Higgins

Copyright 2012, 2013, 2014, 2015

Eden Valley Enterprises
1250 East River St.
Elyria, Ohio 44035

© 2012, 2013, 2014, 2015

All rights reserved.
ISBN:
ISBN-978-1-98-297098-7

Grandma Gatewood: Ohio's Legendary Hiker

Written and Researched By
Kelly Boyer Sagert
and Bette Lou Higgins

Timeline Compiled by Marjorie L. Wood
Bibliography collated by Kay Hoebake and
Bette Lou Higgins
Cover Design by John Lionti
Inside Cover Picture from the collection of
Lillian Gatewood Sullivan
Additional Pictures: Tina Crawford and
Bette Lou Higgins,
Peter Huston and Presley Patrick

TABLE OF CONTENTS

ROLL CREDITS!

The story of Emma Gatewood is a remarkable story on many levels. She is a woman who grew up in a poor family in Appalachia, lived through the Great Depression, survived an abusive relationship and, in the final decades of her life, went on to become a long distance hiker and celebrity and helped to create Ohio's Buckeye Trail.

This book is one section of a multi-part project taken on by Eden Valley Enterprises and FilmAffects. We have already produced a storytelling program about Emma, which is available for bookings. As of this writing, we are working to create a documentary about her life.

Meeting and talking to Emma's relatives and working with Peter Huston of FilmAffects is a once-in-a-lifetime opportunity. We know you'll find Emma's story a once-in-a-lifetime adventure as well!

We have had a lot of help along the way in putting the storytelling program and book together. It would be impossible to list here ALL the people who have provided various forms of help and support so far – but we are grateful to each and every one of them! However, we must mention the following people and organizations that have been instrumental in bringing the project along thus far:

Our funders:
The Buckeye Trail Association, The National
Storytelling Network and the Ohio Humanities Council

Our Individual Contributors:
Our Kickstarter and Individual Donor list can be found
on our Project Web Page (which is updated regularly) at:
http://www.edenvalleyenterprises.org/progdesc/gatewood/
gtwdinf.htm

Special Thanks to:
Nelson Gatewood, Lillian Gatewood Sullivan, Lucy
    Seeds, Marjorie Lynn Wood and all of Emma's
    relatives who have shared information with us.
Michael Higgins, Kay Hoebake, Peter Huston, Lucy &
    Bob Seeds, Pat Thomas and Marjorie Lynn Wood for
    editing assistance.
The Eden Valley Board: Josephine Davis, Michael
    Higgins, Sandra Hines, Margaret Huntley and
    William O'Brien.
Liz McQuaid who started this whole project off and all
    the numerous people who have offered assistance in
    many ways since this project began in 2009.

Enjoy this story and thank you for joining us on the trail
of bringing Emma's story to a wider audience!

Always,
– *i Bette Lou Higgins ! –*

And

Sincerely,
Kelly Boyer Sagert

March 2012

September 1, 2014 Project Update

Since this book was first published this project has
grown! In August of 2013 we held the premier of a one
-act play about Emma. *Trail Magic* by Kelly Boyer
Sagert was first performed at TrueNorth Cultural Arts
in Sheffield Village, Ohio on August 24, 2013.

As of this writing we are raising funds to complete a
PBS documentary about Grandma Gatewood. We have
been awarded a $15,000 Challenge Grant from the Ohio
History Fund for the project. We anticipate the
documentary having its first showing on May 29, 2015
at TrueNorth Cultural Arts.

I invite you to visit our website for complete information
about the project and a schedule of upcoming
performances of our storytelling program, GRANDMA
GATEWOOD: OHIO'S LEGENDARY HIKER and the

play, TRAIL MAGIC. (http://
www.edenvalleyenterprises.org/progdesc/gatewood/
gtwdinf.htm)

I look forward to seeing you at a presentation soon!

– ¡ Bette Lou Higgins ! –
Bette Lou Higgins
Artistic Director
Eden Valley Enterprises

November 24, 2015 Project Update

Our long-awaited documentary about Grandma
Gatewood had its Red Carpet premier on Friday, May
29, 2015 at TrueNorth Cultural Arts. The movie played
to two sold out crowds who enjoyed a reception and
talk-back in between the two film showings.

The two day event, produced by Eden Valley Enterprises
and FilmAffects and hosted by TrueNorth, started
Thursday night, May 28, with a presentation of
GRANDMA GATEWOOD: OHIO'S LEGENDARY
HIKER. I was excited to present this storytelling
program for the evening's festivities which were
underwritten by The National Storytelling Network and
The Parkhurst Brothers, Inc. and was a 2015 NSN
Regional Spotlight Event. Audience members got a look
at Emma's life and accomplishments and enjoyed a Q&A
session afterward. It was the perfect background for the

"rest of the story" that would come with the documentary showing.

On Friday, the film, TRAIL MAGIC: THE GRANDMA GATEWOOD STORY, played to two full houses and was attended by Emma's great-granddaughter, Marjorie Wood, who shared information on-screen and off about her grandmother's life. Marjorie came to the two-day event to help celebrate the culmination of this six year project. Later she wrote to us: "The premier of the PBS documentary was much more than I could imagine! Bette Lou, Peter and Kelly did a wonderful job telling Grandma's story. Anne McEvoy, did an amazing job portraying Grandma. Peter is a fabulous film maker and made her come to life through film. Bette Lou and Kelly told her story through words. There were so many people that work[ed] hard the last six years to make this documentary a reality. Now, Grandma's story can been seen by a new generation of people."

With the film, the play, the storytelling program and this e-book, we have come to the end of our trail to document this feisty female's life. Now we begin a new trail to share her story with a larger audience! I invite you to visit our website regularly to keep up-to-date on where one of these programs will be presented next and come join us if you can! In the meantime, enjoy reading her story.

– ¡ Bette Lou Higgins ! –
Bette Lou Higgins
Artistic Director
Eden Valley Enterprises
(http://www.edenvalleyenterprises.org/progdesc/
gatewood/gtwdinf.htm)

May 23, 2018 Project Update

I am so happy to tell you that "Trail Magic, the
Grandma Gatewood Story" was nominated on April 27,
2017 for a Regional National Association of Television
Arts and Sciences (NATAS) Emmy Award in the "Best
Documentary, Historical" category. Though we did not
win, the nomination was a great honor and we're happy
that we've been able to share Emma's story with so
many! As of this writing, our programs have been seen
by more than 6,900 people (not counting the television
audiences) and more presentations are already scheduled.

Many people have been asking, "What's next now that
your Grandma Gatewood project is done?" It was a
difficult decision — so many stories to choose from!
But after much discussion, we have chosen to spotlight
Victoria Woodhull as our next Feisty Female.

Don't know who Victoria Woodhull is? Well, here's a
short introduction —

Victoria Woodhull (September 23, 1838-June 10, 1927) is truly one of Ohio's most remarkable characters. Coming from a poverty-stricken background and with little education, she managed to become the first woman to publicly address the United States Congress, first woman to run for U.S. president, was an active suffragist, newspaper editor and stockbroker -- she accomplished more than anyone would have expected.

Writer Kelly Boyer Sagert will again be writing our script and Director Peter Huston will be handling the filming duties. Huston calls this "... a great story." and Sagert says that she "... has been fascinated by Victoria Woodhull for decades and is thrilled with the opportunity to delve into Woodhull's rich and complex life."

I hope you will come meet Victoria when we're ready to make the introductions. As always, you can keep track of our programs on our website.

From the Appalachian Trail to the Campaign Trail we're bringing you the stories that others forget!

– *i Bette Lou Higgins !* –
Bette Lou Higgins
Artistic Director
Eden Valley Enterprises
(www.edenvalleyenterprises.org/)

වවව

Meet our next feisty female —

Victoria Woodhull!

Drawing
by Mary McHale for
Eden Valley Enterprises.
Copyright 1999

GRANDMA GATEWOOD:
OHIO'S LEGENDARY HIKER

"Oh, beautiful, for spacious skies, for amber waves of grain..." It was September 25, 1955. Emma Gatewood stood at the top of Mt. Katahdin singing triumphantly. Grandma Gatewood had just become the first woman to thru-hike the Appalachian Trail ALONE! 2,050 miles, 145 days and 30 pounds ago, Emma had left Mt. Oglethorpe, Georgia. But her journey to the top began 67 years before.

On October 25, 1887 Emma Rowena Caldwell was born "...in a ... house back of Mercerville about a mile from where the creeks fork." That's located in Gallia County, close to the Ohio River in the southernmost part of the state. A hop, skip and jump from West Virginia, really.

When Emma was born, there were about 2,000 people living in the whole township – and it might have felt as though Emma's family was half of it! The "puny" log house held her father, Hugh, her mother, Esther Evelyn, and 15 children, including Emma.[1] The children slept four to a bed and sometimes the snow on the roof would tumble through the rafters and give them an "extra blanket."

Life was never easy for Emma. It seemed to be filled with endless chores – hoeing the corn, planting the beans and pumpkins, and worming and suckering the tobacco. She milked the cows; washed dishes; made sausage, lard and head cheese; mended and washed clothes; and cooked. When she and her siblings had a little spare time, they'd wade in the creek, play ball or go sled riding. In 1906, she worked as a housemaid for six weeks. Then, she moved to her Aunt Alice Pickett's house where she did the milking, washing, ironing and cleaning; she shelled corn for the chickens and brought in the coal and kindling wood. For that, she earned 75 cents per week. She had enough time left over to attend Blessing School in Northup, Ohio that only went through the eighth grade. Whenever she got the chance, Emma repeated the eighth grade courses to get in as much education as she could.

When she was living at the Pickett house, she met a young man named Perry Clayton Gatewood who liked to be called P.C. She would ride behind him on a horse and, one time, she fell off because she wasn't bold enough to put her arms around him to hang on. He brought Emma to his house several times and then told her he wanted to get married. She put him off for two months and then he said that, if she wouldn't get married right away, he was leaving to go out West. So, she said yes. Nineteen-year-old Emma and twenty-seven -year-old Perry were married on Sunday, May 5, 1907.

She soon realized that P.C. had browbeaten her to get married; something, she said, that he did lots of times throughout their life together.

Right after their marriage, Emma said, P.C. treated her like a possession, a convenience. He expected her to do everything he wished: building fences, burning tobacco beds, mixing cement or what have you. Emma recalled that he started abusing her three months later and it got steadily worse as long as she lived with him – which was about 33 more years. He started by using an open hand and then his fists – and sometimes his feet. Emma would be black and blue everywhere except her face. This treatment first started when she was pregnant, so Emma felt it was too late to return to her mother. P.C. had a maniacal temper but would act all innocent, pretending that he hadn't touched Emma and telling her that she wasn't in her right mind. He managed to convince a lot of people that she was crazy.

In 1913, the couple bought 80 acres of farmland for $1,000. Emma hauled rocks, picked apples, gathered hay, worked in the tobacco fields and milked the cows – all while she took care of her growing family, which would eventually include eleven children.[2] In 1918, the Gatewoods bought a $30,000 farm near Crown City, Ohio, which they kept until 1938. At that time, she left for California to stay with her mother, feeling as though she could no longer deal with Perry's cruel behavior. Her face had been beaten out of recognition ten times that year. Eventually, she came home and P.C. had a big homecoming for her. Most of his family came for a pot-luck dinner on the lawn. But in September 1940, P.C. beat Emma so badly that she finally got a divorce. Even though her marriage did not work out, she loved her children.

Besides raising the children, Emma was responsible for helping to plant vegetables and to work in the field on their farm. If any flowers got planted, that was up to Emma, too. Lots of farmers don't like flowers and think they're nothing but a nuisance – but flowers were important to her, important enough that she'd get up at 4 a.m. to work in the flower beds by the light of a kerosene lantern before breakfast was due at 6. Then there was the canning and cooking and cleaning and all. Emma would dry fruits and vegetables on top of the smokehouse roof. When it was berry picking time, the children would pick them; Emma would stay up all night canning – and then start her routine all over again in the morning.

Emma was a strict disciplinarian who taught her children to live by the Golden Rule every day, not just on Sundays. If one of them ever said, "But I can't do that," Emma would always reply that "can't never <u>did</u> anything." She taught them not to waste – and then to learn to do with what they had, and be happy with it. She felt that people too often patterned themselves after others instead of being individuals. Too many of us don't have the strength of character to stand alone, she would say, while some of us also have habits that weaken our bodies, our morals and our minds – drinking, chewing tobacco, smoking, swearing and drinking coffee.

She taught her children to work hard – and not to go crybabying around if life didn't go their way. Emma allowed them to have fun sometimes, too. If P.C. needed to be away from home for the night, for example, she'd let the kids push the furniture out of the way and play Blind Man's Bluff. That was always a special treat.

When it was time to wash blankets and quilts, Emma would get a big washtub, fill it up with water and blankets – and then put her kids on top. They had so much pep that they were like a human washing machine as they kicked and squirmed around – and they had so much fun that they didn't know they were doing chores. Meanwhile, Emma could go attend to something else, since laundry was being done. With a family as big as hers – and a farm that needed so much attention – you had to do two or three things at once, or you'd never get anything done. That same old tub worked just fine as a bathtub in the summer, too. Emma would fill it up with water and let the children splash around.

It was a good thing that Emma didn't get sick very often because she wouldn't have had the time to be ill. She only went into town once or twice a year, and one of those times was for Christmas shopping. Emma always wanted to make sure that everybody got one or two gifts, maybe costing 10 or 15 cents each. After her holiday shopping trip one year, Emma got sick and needed to go to bed – that's how bad she felt. Her daughter Esther wrapped the presents for everyone. Esther was about 12 years old at the time and was excited to be the one who knew what was in every package.

People from town would come to Emma for a cure whenever they were ailing. She had a great big doctor book and would try to help folks out. When she couldn't, she'd tell them to go to a real doctor. Sometimes they'd protest: "But we want you, Emma!"

Once, her daughter Esther broke her arm in two different places. Emma and P.C. sent her to a proper doctor and her arm was set in wooden splints. He charged the family two whole dollars. The thing is, Esther had been working in the fields and was all dirty before she broke her bone – and the doctor hadn't even bothered to wash her up first. So, when the Gatewoods got home, Emma unwrapped the splint, cleaned her up and then reset it. The arm healed just fine, too.

Then, there was the time that her daughter, Rowena, cut off the tip of her finger. Emma wasn't quite sure what to do, so she put it back in place with a splint and bandaged it all up and it grew back the way it was supposed to.

Apparently, Emma got her doctoring skills from her mother. When Emma was young, she was sitting by a fire and the wind blew the flames towards her, catching her clothes on fire. She was burned fairly badly. Her mother applied soothing medicine using a feather. Her mother needed to be very gentle as the burns were painful – but, thankfully, they did heal. Later Emma passed the skill to her daughter, Esther. Once, Esther got an infected blister on her hand. It was so bad that she couldn't sleep, so she took her father's straight razor, sterilized it and lanced the blister herself. When Emma saw her, she asked Esther what she was doing. Emma listened, and then just told her daughter to be careful and to soak it every so often (she used Lifebuoy soap) until it healed.

Emma kept a list of home remedies that she collected and shared with others. She wrote: "I had an Aunt that made her children black hen manure tea for measles. Sassafras tea to thin the blood… When children had worms they would use castor oil with a few drops of turpentine… for boils etc. we used soap, fat meat, bread and milk, [juices of] chew of tobacco …"

Besides being well known for her homeopathic remedies, Emma also earned a reputation as an excellent quilter and rug maker.

When she was younger, Emma worked from sunup to sundown and seldom had time to herself – so reading was a real pleasure. On July 7, 1954 Grandma was relaxing by reading a 1949 issue of *National Geographic*. One of the articles featured Earl Schaffer, the first person to ever hike the entire Appalachian Trail (A.T.) in one trip. The writer went on to say that, to date, only five men had ever hiked the entire trail by themselves – and no woman ever had. Emma, who loved a challenge, began thinking about tackling that trail. After all, she was now a "free woman." Her children were grown and she was only responsible for herself. Why NOT hike the Appalachian Trail?

The Appalachian Trail is about 2,181-miles long [3] through the Appalachian Mountains containing dense forests, rocky mountains with spectacular views and crystal clear lakes. At the time, the trail went from Mount Oglethorpe, Georgia to Mount Katahdin, Maine. Mountains are measured by how many feet the peak is above sea level. Mount Oglethorpe is 3,169 feet above sea level. Mount Katahdin [4] is the highest mountain in the whole state of Maine at 5,268 feet.

Only about fifteen percent of the people who try to hike the entire trail in one season succeed – and most travel in decent-sized groups, not all alone. It usually takes about five months to hike through the fourteen states, six national parks and eight national forests along the trail, with the hikers sometimes dealing with snow and, other times, with extremely hot, humid weather.

Although hiking 2,050 miles through rough, often uninhabited, terrain sounds like too big of a challenge for anyone who is 66 years old, male or female, Emma was a strong, independent, determined woman – and so, in July 1954, she decided to try to become the first woman to hike the entire Appalachian Trail by herself. The magazine article had explained that the trail was cleared out well, and was a comfortable four feet in width; food was easy to get, the writer shared, and shelters were within easy walking distance. That didn't sound so bad, Emma thought, even though she had never before climbed a mountain.

Since Emma was divorced and her 11 children were grown, she didn't have to ask anyone's permission or even tell anyone where she was going. That way, none of them could try to stop her or change her mind! Because she wasn't telling anyone what she was doing, she couldn't ask anyone for advice on what to pack. Instead of reading lists about what she should take for such a long hike, she decided to think about what she would actually use and that's how she packed – using plain old common sense.

Emma left her home in Gallipolis, Ohio on July 7, 1954, taking a bus to Pittsburgh, Pennsylvania then to New York. She arrived at Millinocket, Maine on July 9 and started to hike the very next day. She spent her first night in a lean-to near a creek, laying out her blanket on the floor as a mattress. After just one day of hiking, she realized that she had brought too many clothes. Fortunately, she was near York Camp where she could mail most of her clothes back home – and she did. She then walked thirteen more miles to the Rainbow Lake Camp where she stayed for two days. Emma wrote in her diary on July 12, "… The Richards that have the camp were very nice to me and feasted (sic) me on roast beef and pie for free. I got a cabin and had a good night."

Unfortunately, after Emma left that camp, she misread a weather-rotted sign and took a wrong turn. She then could not find her way back to the main trail. Emma searched for an hour and a half and then decided to take a break. She whistled a song, built a fire and dried her clothes. She ate raisins and peanuts to keep up her strength. Emma wrote in her diary that she wasn't worried about being lost. If this was to be the end of her, this was – in Emma's opinion – as good a place as any for that to happen. Having said that, she wasn't about to give up. She searched again for the main trail, briefly finding it before losing it again.

That night, she built another fire and she slept on a rock. The next morning, she kept trying different paths so that she could find the main trail again – but she kept choosing side paths that were worn down by deer and beaver and they all kept leading back to the same pond. Emma built a fire near the pond and put some water on it, thinking that the steam created could serve as smoke signals that would lead rescuers to her. Although that sounded like a great idea, it didn't work.

Emma decided that, since she wasn't going to get rescued any time soon, she might as well take a bath in the pond. She took off her glasses and placed them on a rock – and then stepped on them, breaking one of the lenses. She patched up her glasses with a Band-Aid, but struggled to see out of them. That night, she slept underneath an abandoned boat.

The next morning, she tried creating smoke signals again, without any good results, even when she could see a plane flying overhead. By this time, she was out of food and was surrounded by pesky black flies. Emma decided that she might as well look for the main Appalachian Trail again. This time, she found it near the Rainbow Lake Camp, where she met up with some rangers who had been searching for her. When she started her hike, she needed to sign in and the rangers noticed that she had not returned or been seen for quite a while. Emma told the rangers that she hadn't been lost, only misplaced. The rangers recommended that she give up hiking. Emma agreed, but privately began planning to return the next year and, this time, to start in Georgia and work her way back toward Maine. It seems likely that the rangers never expected to see her again, but Emma had a habit of proving people wrong.

The rangers offered her a plane ride to the train station and she accepted. She went to the Penobscot Hotel where she had stayed before she started her hike and told the boy at the desk she had been climbing mountains. When she got into her room, she looked into the mirror and saw her reflection for the first time since she had started her hike. She saw a woman with broken, patched up glasses; a black eye that she had somehow sustained on the trail; and a sweater full of holes. She laughed at her appearance and, in her diary, wrote, "... I looked worse than a drunk out of the gutter. I had to laugh at myself."

Before heading home, she bought a new outfit. Later, she simply told people that she had climbed Mount Katahdin. She didn't mention that her original plan had been to hike the entire Appalachian Trail – or that she had gotten lost so early in her quest.

Now, it would be perfectly understandable if Emma decided not to try to hike the entire Appalachian Trail again after such an aggravating and frightening first attempt. Emma was not a quitter, though, and so, again, without telling her family, she made plans for her second hiking trip the next year.

During that time, Emma helped take care of a neighbor's wife who was ill. She wrote in her diary that she went to the hospital every day and walked "... over and back three times each way and doing the work at the house. … I got exercise walking up and down stairs for my [next] trip on the trail." [5]

Her family certainly wouldn't have suspected that Emma was away if they'd gone through her house in the spring of 1955. She had learned plenty last year about traveling light on the A.T. All she took with her for her second attempt were the essentials, including a blanket, a plastic shower sheet, a cup, a canteen and baby bottle for water, a small pot, a spoon, a Swiss Army knife, a first aid kit, pins, a flashlight, a piece of rope, a raincoat, a warm coat and a change of clothes. She didn't take a compass, a guidebook of the trail, a tent, a sleeping bag or a backpack. That's traveling light!

Emma wore plain old tennis shoes that she'd bought at Carl's Shoe Store in Gallipolis. For food, Emma took along dried beef, cheese and nuts – and she planned to find fruits growing wild along the way to supplement her meals. She used a walking stick of sassafras and carried candied mints in case she got an upset stomach.

On May 2, 1955, Emma – who had never learned how to drive – traveled with a friend as far as Charleston, West Virginia, where she planned to take a train to Georgia. When she found out that the train didn't leave until the next morning, she walked to a hotel where she could buy a plane ticket. She took the bus to the airport and flew to Atlanta, where she tried to get a ride to Mount Oglethorpe and was told that there was no such place. After Emma took out a map and pointed out the mountain, a cab driver agreed to take her as far as one quarter of a mile from the peak for a fee of five dollars. She paid him – but then the driver complained the whole time that he wasn't making any money from this fare, so Emma gave him an extra dollar so that he would be quiet.

Once Emma made it to the mountain, she tossed a home-sewn denim sack with her clothes over her shoulder and set off. In 1955, 850 miles of the Appalachian Trail was adjacent to private property so, for more than one third of her hike, she would be only a few miles from homes and farms.

After hiking for several miles, she stopped at a nearby house to ask for a drink. She thought they considered her a bit wacky, but they did give her some water. That first day, she walked fifteen miles, including two miles off the main trail. She found a farmhouse where she could spend the night.

She didn't find a place where she could sleep indoors the next night. She did find a pile of large cardboard boxes which she used to make a bed. As she tried to rest, a mouse kept running around her. Emma tried to scare the mouse away, but it didn't scare easily and, in fact, it kept her up most of the night.

The next day Emma was thrilled to find a good spring

where she could take a long drink, wash some clothes and take a partial bath. That night, she filled her sack with leaves and used it as a mattress on top of a picnic table.

As she became accustomed to the trail, she appreciated the things of beauty that she saw – colorful azaleas, sweet smelling shrubs, a pink dogwood tree or deer with their white tails held up high. She met people who offered her good buttermilk and cornbread or gave her a ride into a nearby town where she could buy provisions and eat a hot meal.

One night, she stayed with a woman named Mrs. Wilkins, who had 17 children. Mrs. Wilkins and one of her daughters chewed tobacco, which amused Emma. Another night, Emma asked a woman whose hair looked as though it hadn't been combed in weeks if she could spend the night at her farmhouse. The woman said they never turned anyone away. Emma was a bit nervous about staying there, though, as the woman's apron was so dirty that it looked as though it could stand up all by itself. Her face was grimy. The house was filthy. Emma's dilemma was resolved when the man of the house kicked Emma out when he found out that she hadn't told her family where she was.

Yet another time, Emma knocked on the door of a cabin. When an older man answered, she asked if he had any food, and he invited her in. There was a big pot of beans simmering on his stove and she watched him retrieve a tin plate from his sink. That was okay, but then he wiped the plate with a dishrag that was so dirty that it was black; he wiped off a spoon with that same filthy rag. Although the rag certainly captured Emma's attention, she ate the beans, thinking that, "If it hasn't killed him, it won't kill me."

Things didn't always go smoothly along the trail. She lost her knife and her matches wouldn't light. Fortunately, her matches dried out and, a couple of days later, she visited a store where she could replace her pocket knife. The next day, her walking stick broke and she needed to be on the lookout for a good replacement. Luckily, she found one. Soon after that, she had another stroke of good luck. She was quite thirsty and didn't have water when she saw a garbage lid that was bent enough to have captured some rain water. She drank that water and then used the lid to catch some more rain.

Emma didn't have a map – and she definitely didn't want to get lost on this trip – so she carefully followed the white blaze marks along the trail. A blaze is a painted rectangle placed in a prominent location. The 2 by 6 inch white blazes indicated the Appalachian Trail itself; side trails and trails that led to shelters used blue blazes. If Emma saw two white blazes, one above the other, she was alerted to watch for an unusual turn or route change. By following the blazes, Emma was able to stay on – or easily return to – the main trail.

There were still plenty of practical matters that she
needed to figure out, though. For one thing, there
weren't any toilets along the trail – although sometimes
there were outhouses if she went off-trail to a shelter.
Whenever she needed to relieve herself and there wasn't
a toilet around, she had to go at least 80 paces away
from the main trail and make sure that she was also
away from any natural source of water or any form of
shelter. She would then dig a hole that was six to eight
inches deep; use that hole as a toilet; and then cover it
up. There weren't many showers available, either, except
for the occasional one off-trail in a shelter. When she
needed to clean herself, Emma had to collect water from
a stream or lake; carry it about 200 feet away from the
source of water; and then rinse herself off.

When Emma needed a drink, she seldom came across a
water faucet or pump. She had to keep an eye out for
springs or streams. Unfortunately, some dried up
during the hot summer and early fall. The water might
look, smell and taste good, but it could also contain
bacteria that could cause digestive problems. If she
wanted to kill off the bacteria, she needed to boil her
water.

Blisters can be a big problem for hikers. To avoid them,
Emma would take off her shoes and socks when resting
to let her feet dry out. Another problem was bad

weather. Emma needed to watch the sky and try to be near shelter during hard rains. On the northern part of the trail, in Maine, it can snow any time of the year – and so she risked hypothermia, even when the weather was above freezing. She also needed to stay hydrated in hot weather to avoid heat cramps, heat exhaustion or heat stroke.

Emma needed to be careful along the way or she might get sick from ticks, mouse droppings and animal bites. She also had to be on the lookout for things like poison ivy.

Wherever she went, Emma needed to watch out for snakes. On May 29, 1955, Emma wrote in her diary, "I started at six thirty after a fairly good night. ...The sun was hot and I was poking about up Turkey Bald Mt. (N.C.) when I heard a noise which I thot *(sic)* was a bird of some kind. I felt something hit my dungarees and looked down and saw a large rattler coiled. I had my cane ready to put down, and it went between the snake's head and me. I gave a jump sideways, and went on without being bitten. It was the first rattler I had seen on my trip." During the first 1,500 miles of her hike, she saw three copperheads and two rattlesnakes. That's a whole lot of snake poison! [6]

Perhaps one of the biggest dangers, though, was running into a black bear that was either startled or protecting cubs. To prevent bears from being attracted to campsites, hikers are advised to hang their water bottles, food and cookware in a strong tree branch at least ten feet off the ground, at least 200 feet from any campsite – not an easy task. Another potential problem for Emma was falling, twisting an ankle or otherwise injuring herself to the point that she couldn't keep walking. Then she would be at the mercy of other hikers – IF she happened to meet one in time.

One of the biggest physical challenges on the hike was the Hundred-Mile Wilderness in Maine. There are no roads that intersect that part of the trail, so she wouldn't be able to arrange to have any supplies brought in to her. She would be able to eat only what she could carry or what she could scrounge up. As Emma put it, "This wasn't a trail! It was a nightmare." Also in Maine was a dreaded one-mile-long canyon filled with boulders called the Mahoosuc Notch. This canyon featured dangerous ten-foot drops; pockets of slick ice (even in July!); and other features that challenged even the most experienced hikers – and Emma had to tackle that treacherous mile as well.

Throughout her journey she crawled over rocks slick with sleet and she needed to cross 30-foot swollen streams. She dug her way through dense underbrush and crawled through holes in rocks. She would sleep anywhere she could lie down, sometimes outside and sometimes in a house, if the owner didn't slam the door in her face. She slept on porch swings, under picnic tables and on porch floors, in abandoned lean-tos, in old camps and in piles of leaves. Sometimes, she'd even heat up rocks and sleep on them. There were horribly burned out areas on the trail and sand washouts. There were tall, nearly impassable weeds and unusable shelters that were blown down, burned down or utterly filthy.

Hikers need to be resourceful – and Emma definitely was. When the dreaded black flies struck, she remembered her farm training when horses were given a hat of sassafras leaves to keep the flies away. So Emma found a sassafras branch, stuck the sweet scented stick inside her visor and let it hang down over her ears. When she found a discarded rubber heel from a man's shoe, she taped it over her own to reinforce it; when Emma needed a comb, she broke off the handle of a used picnic fork that she'd found and used that in her hair. When she found an abandoned sheepskin coat, she turned it into a vest for herself; when she saw a pair of abandoned gloves, she took them with her. Yet another time, she saw campers toss something in the trash. She looked to see if it was anything valuable and found an unopened loaf of bread and some apples and oranges.

Whenever she needed a snack, she ate wild huckleberries or she'd make a salad of sorts from sorrel. [7] It also helped to suck on bouillon cubes because it kept enough salt in her body. It was fortunate that she knew lots of herbal treatments so she could treat herself any time she felt a little poorly.

Sometimes, Emma would meet up with other hikers on the trail, some friendly, others – not so much. She met up with one miserly old man who refused to even share a drink of water with her. Fortunately, she also met a wonderful woman who gave her fried chicken to eat on the trail. Another man shared some pan-fried trout, a treat that she had never enjoyed before.

Emma hiked with a steady gait and she disliked it if anyone ever passed her up – and she let them know that she disliked it, too! Sometimes she'd meet a scout group and she would hike with them.

On August 11 she came to a shelter where she met Harold Bell, who had just gotten out of the Navy, and Steve Sargent, who had been at the US Naval Academy. Since it was raining out, the three of them settled in for the night. They made a fire, had dinner and conversation. When it was time for bed, they hung a blanket divider.

Several days later, she came to Clarendon Gorge. It was pretty wide, pretty broad, and the water was rushing fairly fast. As she started trying to figure out how she was going to get across, Harold and Steve showed up! They tied her between them and one of them carried her pack. They waded her across that wide, broad, rushing creek. Right in the middle, she got seasick so she looked away from the water and wondered – "How did an old woman like me get caught up into a situation like this?"

During her hike, Emma talked to many people and eventually her story came to the attention of some reporters. Nearly midway through her trek, Emma found out that one of the papers would be running a story about her, so she quickly sent her children postcards so they wouldn't hear about their mother's adventure by reading the news. She later learned that Esther received her postcard just one day before the story appeared in the press – and Esther wasn't especially surprised at the news, since she knew her mother always had a mind of her own.

On September 22, Emma fell and broke a lens in her glasses. The following day, she hiked to Rainbow Lake Camp in Maine, the same place where, in 1954, she had ended her attempt to hike the entire trail – in large part because her glasses were broken! Emma recorded in her diary that the people at the camp were quite surprised to see her again and they treated her like royalty and her glasses were repaired.

While on this hike, Emma witnessed areas of pure beauty. The lakes that she saw in the Hundred-Mile Wilderness were lovely and the songs of the birds kept her company. Ultimately, Emma successfully tackled all of the challenges on the trail, becoming the first woman to hike the entire Appalachian Trail ALONE! On

September 25, 1955, Emma reached the final mountain peak in Maine, after hiking 2,050 miles in 145 days. It was so windy that she feared being blown off the mountaintop! She sang a verse of *America the Beautiful* and signed the register book to record her presence.

Hiking 2,000-plus miles caused Emma's feet to expand from a size 8C to 8D and to wear out six pairs of shoes. When Emma was in Damascus, Virginia, she visited with the mayor, Elizabeth McKee. They chatted and drank ice tea. Then Grandma bought a new pair of red ball jet shoes [8] and left her old ones with the mayor.

Emma told a newspaper reporter that she had expected the trip to be a nice lark – but it wasn't. Had she known how tough hiking the entire trail was going to be, she wouldn't have started. However, once she did, she was determined not to quit. She said that she tried to hike the entire trail this time so that she could see all that she missed in 1954.

Emma Gatewood had just accomplished something that sounded impossible – and at the relatively old age of 67. Emma's response? "Most people are pantywaists. Exercise is good for you."

Of course, Emma was not the type of woman who rested on her laurels or who backed away from a challenge. Therefore, it shouldn't be surprising to learn that, after completing her now-famous A.T. hike, she returned in 1957 for a second thru-hike. In 1958, she climbed the six highest peaks of the Adirondack Mountains of New York.

In 1959, she decided to hike behind a wagon train traveling between Independence, Missouri to Portland, Oregon. Her plan was to walk along the 2,000-mile Oregon Trail to honor the Oregon Centennial. By the time she got to Missouri, though, she found out that the wagon train had left without her.

Map from The Ox Team, or the Old Oregon Trail 1852–1906, by Ezra Meeker; from Wikipedia
picture in Public domain in the United States
https://en.wikipedia.org/wiki/Route_of_the_Oregon_Trail

Emma had a couple of choices. She could turn around and go home – but, she wasn't much of a quitter. Or, she could start hiking, and that's what she did. It was often hot and windy, so she covered her mouth to make it easier to keep breathing AND to make it more difficult for those skunks with cameras – her inelegant name for photographers – to take her picture! She hated how people always wanted her to stop and pose for pictures. If she stopped for all of them, she declared, she'd never get to Portland. When some of them got rude with her about taking a photo, she got rude right back.

When the hike was almost over, the deputy sheriff of the region offered to carry her umbrella for the rest of the hike, but she told him not on his life because she needed it to defend herself from "commoners with cameras." Finally, after hiking the whole 2,000 miles, she found out that she'd reached the end, in Portland, before the wagon train! Emma had averaged about 22 miles per day – and it was awfully tempting to head back to cheer the wagon train on. Ends up that she finished the hike a full week before the wagon train crossed the finish line!

By this time, she was really tired of the newspaper reporters and photographers following her around, tired of all the fuss that goes along with being a celebrity. One of them actually asked her if this hike was a publicity stunt for money! "Phooey on you" was about the nicest thing she could think of to say to a reporter like that.

She did get into a bit of trouble with a photographer named Robert Hall. She was weary of walking on the trail, so she sat down to rest. Who shows up right on the trail? This   reporter and a radio man! They talked to Emma for a bit, which was fine with her, but then one of them aimed his camera at her. She finally had enough. She hit him on the forehead with her blue umbrella. Bob's forehead bled and she just sat there and cried. It took someone offering her a hamburger and a glass of cold water for her to calm down. Later Bob was quoted as saying, "She hits like a mule."

People apparently forgave her, though, because Governor Hatfield made her an ambassador-at-large of the Oregon Centennial Celebration and she got the keys to the cities of Portland, Medford and Seaside. In her honor, any woman, aged 65 or older, who attended Oregon Centennial festivities got in for free. As for her blue umbrella (which cost $1.50!) – it became a permanent exhibit at the Portland Historical Museum.

In 1964, she hiked the Appalachian Trail by herself again, making her the first person to hike that trail three times – man or woman – although, the last time, she needed to do it in sections, being well into her 70s by this point. On one of Emma's follow-up hikes on the A.T., an older man asked if he could hike with her. She refused, saying that, "People might talk."

Emma received a lot of attention for what she did, being interviewed by *Sports Illustrated* and appearing on the "Today Show" in New York City with Dave Garroway and on the Jack Smith show, "Welcome Traveler." She got a letter from Groucho Marx and a cable from Art Linkletter, and she appeared on both of their shows, too. Thanks to all of the attention she got, she was even able to visit 48 of the 50 states, all except Alaska and Hawaii. And, to top it all, her name became part of the Congressional Records when Ohio Congressman Thomas Jenkins gave a speech to the US Congress commending her hiking achievements!

Right around the time that she finished her second complete hike of the Appalachian Trail, Emma joined the National Campers and Hikers Association and she would walk to meetings held in Columbus, Ohio. It was through this group that, around 1959, she met people who were interested in forming a trail system for the state of Ohio. She and thirteen other people became the executive committee of the Buckeye Trail Association. Emma worked hard to help the association achieve its goals and the trail officially came into being on June 17, 1959. Thirty-five people participated in the first official Buckeye Trail Association hike and Emma served as the honored dignitary.

The original plan was to have the Buckeye Trail run east from Cincinnati, parallel to the Ohio River; pass through Emma's home county of Gallia; then run north to Conneaut by Lake Erie. This plan wasn't feasible because it cut through too much private land, so the official route went through Hocking County, over publicly held land, rather than through Gallia.

Emma nevertheless arranged an unofficial loop of the trail that was between 35 and 40 miles in length that went from one corner of Gallia County to the other. She secured permission from landowners, cleared away brush and helped to create a decent path for hikers.

Emma donated $20 so that the association could buy the first blue paint needed to create navigational blazes on the Buckeye Trail. There had been some discussion about the color of the blazes on the Buckeye Trail. Should they be blue, because of how well it contrasts against the green and brown colors of the trees or should they be white, as they are on the Appalachian Trail? Ultimately, blue was chosen, in part because it's an easier color to see when snow coats the tree trunks.

Emma was elected to the Buckeye Trail Association board of directors, and she served through April 1969, by which time she had hiked ten thousand miles! When she retired from active service, she was named the Director Emeritus and was granted an honorary lifetime membership to the association. She was honored for her initiative and perseverance in planning and developing a significant section of the trail; for the recognition and honor she brought to the organization by her association with it; and for the guidance and advice that she so readily shared. Emma also received a State Conservation Award from Ohio Governor James Rhodes.

Around 1961, Emma led a six-mile hike on the Buckeye Trail in the Hocking Hills State Park. The group walked by Old Man's Cave, Cedar Falls and Ash Cave. The hike that she led was named the Winter Hike and it was repeated every year in January for the next 12 years. As she aged, she sometimes needed to be helped and even carried over the rough spots, but she kept participating. When the 1973 hike was being planned, though, organizers recognized that, for the first time, Emma was not strong enough to lead the hike, even with assistance. So, they made her the official hostess that year. Her job was to greet hikers as they arrived and organizers held the 1973 Winter Hike in her honor.

In 1979, the Buckeye Trail Association named part of their trail the Grandma Gatewood Trail and Congress certified this section as a National Recreational Trail. Besides being part of the Buckeye Trail, the Grandma Gatewood Trail is also part of the 4,600-mile federal North Country Trail that runs from New York to North Dakota and part of the 6,800-mile American Discovery Trail that goes from California to Delaware.

Cedar Falls

On June 3, 1973, at the age of 85, Emma Gatewood suffered a heart attack. The next day in the hospital, she awoke from a coma, hummed a bit of "Mine Eyes Have Seen the Glory (of the coming of the Lord)," closed her eyes and passed away.

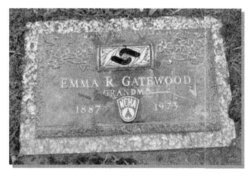

According to her son Nelson, Emma said the hardest part of hiking the Appalachian Trail was simply making up her mind to do it – and that's a lesson that we can all take to heart, no matter what we want to achieve.

In 1999, the 1,400-mile Buckeye Trail was named Ohio's Millennium Legacy Trail by the U.S. Department of Transportation. Only one trail can receive this award per state. Surely this would have pleased Emma Gatewood, a woman who loved nature and the beauty of the earth, a woman with courage, determination and fortitude, a woman who knew her own mind and acted upon it, whether or not it was the typical thing for a woman of her age to do. The next time that you go on a walk and see glorious trees, streams and wildlife and you take in a lungful of fresh clean air, think about "Grandma" Emma Rowena Caldwell Gatewood and how she left this world a better place.

Many words have been written ABOUT Emma. Here are some of HER words. She loved writing poetry. This one is called "The Reward Of Nature"

If you will go with me to the mountains
And sleep on the leaf-carpeted floors
And enjoy the bigness of nature
And the beauty of all out-of-doors.

You will find your troubles all fading
And feel the creator was not man
That made the lovely mountains and forests
Which only a supreme power can.

When we trust in the power above
And with the realm of nature hold fast
We will have a jewel of great price
To brighten our lives till the last.

For the love of nature is healing
If we will only give it a try.
And the reward will be forthcoming
If we go deeper than what meets the eye.

"The Reward of Nature" was written by Emma Gatewood and generously provided by the family.

಄಄಄

FOOTNOTES

1. Emma's father enlisted in The Civil War on December 1, 1863 and served as a private in Company D, 9th West Virginia infantry. He was apparently wounded at the Battle of Cedar Creek. He later lost his leg apparently due to a war injury. Emma's siblings were: John, Thomas, Alfred, Bert and David, Etta, Edith, Ethel, Alta, Ella, Effie, Myrtie, Ida Estelle and Lucy.

2. Emma's children were: Helen, Ruth, Monroe, William, Rowena, Esther, Elizabeth, Robert, Nelson, Louise and Lucy. Elizabeth and Robert were twins.

3. The length of the Trail changes from year to year. When Emma hiked the mileage was basically 2,050 miles. The official mileage for 2011 was listed at 2,181. (source: Laurie Potteiger, Information Services Manager, Appalachian Trail Conservancy.)

4. The name "Katahdin" comes from the Penobscot Indians and it means "The Greatest Mountain."

5. Later Emma wrote that all that walking paid off "... for my legs did not bother me when I got on the trail like they would have otherwise."

6. On a subsequent hike, she lay down one night and unconsciously moved her arm and frightened a buzzard that had landed on her. Later she said, "I knew I hadn't had a bath, but I didn't know I was that bad off."

7. Sorrel is a green leaf vegetable native to Europe. It is often called common sorrel or spinach dock. In some cultures it is considered more of an herb than a vegetable.

8. As of October, 2013, her shoes were on display at Mt. Rogers Outfitters, Damascus, Virginia.

&&&

NOTES

🖎 First Completed A.T. Hike: May 3 – September 25, 1955 (2050 Miles; 145 days per Ohioana Honors and Hiking Record) Dates in Ohioana Honors and Hiking Record & "Hiking The Appalachian Trail" by James Hare (A.T. File)

🖎 Second Completed A.T. Hike: April 27 – September 16, 1957 "Hiking The Appalachian Trail" by James Hare (A.T. File)

🖎 The episode with Steve Sargent and Harold Bell was actually a bit more dramatic than any of them realized. As far as they knew, they were in the middle of a rainstorm when, in fact, they were in the midst of a hurricane! From August 11 – 14 Hurricane Connie was covering the area. Clarendon Gorge (which Steve and Harold carried Emma across) was at flood stages and the three of them could have been swept away at any minute. Steve and Harold gave up their hike shortly after that, but Emma kept going. Hurricane Diane caused problems for the hikers from August 17 – 20. (Source: Phone interviews with Harold Bell and Steve Sargent by Bette Lou Higgins, "Hurricane Connie." Wikipedia, the free encyclopedia. http:// en.wikipedia.org/wiki/Hurricane_Connie and "The Floods of Hurricane Connie and Diane." NOAA. http://www.erh.noaa.gov/nerfc/historical/ aug1955.htm)

🖎 Regarding Emma's weight loss and foot changes during the hike: "A Touch Of Sassafras" claims 25 pounds and her feet went up two sizes. "Hiking The Appalachian Trail" by James Hare says 30 pounds and size 8C to 8D. Daughter Lucy Seeds says she was about 5'2" and weighed about 152 BEFORE she lost that 30 pounds on the hike, but she gained most of it back.

ଛ The Grandma Gatewood Trail in Ohio is the section of the Buckeye Trail from Old Man's Cave to Ash Cave in Hocking Hills State Park.

ଛ Old Man's Cave is located off of State Route 664, about 11 miles south of U.S. 33. The cave is about 200 feet long and 50 feet high; it's made of Blackhand sandstone that is 250 million years old. It was named after Richard Rowe, an older man who used to live in the cave. In the area surrounding Old Man's Cave, there are three waterfalls and several pools.

ଛ Ash Cave is located off of State Route 56 and is Ohio's largest recessed cave. The face of this cave is horseshoe-shaped and is 700 feet high; there is a 90-foot-high waterfall located by the cave. It was named after the ash piles found in the cave, which indicate that Native Americans used to spend time in it.

ଛ Between the two caves is Cedar Falls, one of the most beautiful waterfalls in Ohio. Water descends 50 feet into a pool and, in the winter time, the waterfall turns into a huge icicle.

❧ Trees in the area of the hike include eastern hemlocks, the Canada yew and the yellow and black birch. Along the trail, a splendid gorge cuts through the Blackhand sandstone, letting visitors see the glory of the earth's subsurface.

❧ There is also a Grandma Gatewood Trail at Bob Evans Farm in Bidwell, Ohio.

❧❧❧

Emma's Diaries

TIMELINE
Compiled by Marjorie L. Wood

1879 21 October: Perry Clayton Gatewood born, Crown City, Ohio to James Madison & Margaret Sheets Gatewood

1887 25 October: Emma born in Mercerville, Gallia Co., Ohio to Hugh Wilson and Esther Evelyn Trowbridge Caldwell

1907 05 May: Emma married Perry Clayton Gatewood. Emma was 19 years old

1908 22 April: birth of Helen Marie Gatewood

1909 31 December: birth of Ruth Estelle Gatewood

1911 18 June: birth of Ernest Monroe Gatewood

1914 22 January: birth of William Anderson Gatewood

1916 13 April: birth of Rowena Mae Gatewood

1918 23 April: birth of Esther Ann Gatewood

1920 06 August: birth of twins Robert Wilson and Elizabeth Caldwell Gatewood

1923 28 December: birth of Nelson Lewis Gatewood

1926 04 March: birth of Dora Louise Gatewood

1928 28 May: birth of Lucy Eleanor Gatewood

1941 06 February: Emma and Perry divorce

1947: Emma compiled a book of poems and gave it to many family members and close friends that year and in later years

1955: Emma becomes the first woman to hike the Appalachian Trail May 3-Sept 25, distance 2050 miles, 145 days, age 67

1955 10 June: article in *Sports Illustrated*

1955 15 August: article in *Sports Illustrated*

1955 October: appeared on NBC Jack Smith Show, "Welcome Traveler," New York City

1955 October: appeared on Dave Garroway, "Today Show," New York City

1956: A speech by Congressman Jenkins (Ironton, Oh.) to the US Congress commending for her achievement for hiking is placed in the Congressional Records

1956: Emma is made a lifetime member of the National Campers & Hikers Association and received a trophy

1957: Second hike of the Appalachian Trail

1957 August: article in *Norfolk and Western Magazine*

1958: Emma hiked the Adirondacks in New York State, climbed six of the highest mountains, age 70

1958 November: article in *The 65 Magazine*, "A Guide to A Livelier Golden Age"

1959: Emma walked 2,000 miles on the highway from Independence, Missouri to Portland, Oregon for Oregon Centennial, in 95 days, age 71 (May 4 – August 7)

1959: Emma received parchment from Governor Hatfield of Oregon making her a goodwill ambassador at large

1959: Emma received keys to the cities of Portland, Medford and Seaside, Oregon

1959: Clothes Emma wore on the Oregon Trail hike are placed in the museum at Portland, Oregon

1959 August: Emma is interviewed on the "Art

Linkletter Show," Hollywood, CA. A photo of Emma and Art Linkletter appeared in a Los Angeles newspaper.

1959: Huntington, WV WSAZ-TV interview

1959: Boise, Idaho TV interview

1959 November: *The Ohio Conservation Bulletin* mentions her in an article about the Buckeye Trail.

1960: Emma walked the Long Trail in Vermont from Massachusetts to Canada, age 72

1960: Emma walked the Baker Trail in Pennsylvania twice, age 72

1960: Emma walked the Horseshoe Trail in Pennsylvania, age 72

1960: Emma appeared on Groucho Marx "You Bet Your Life" TV show, Hollywood, California

1960 June: article in *The Ohio Conservation Bulletin* magazine

1960 November: Emma sent Buckeye and Pawpaw seeds to the Mayor of Portland, Oregon and she received a letter thanking her for these

1961: WBNS-TV Columbus, Ohio interview

1964: Emma hiked the Appalachian Trail a third time, age 76

1964: Emma started blazing the Buckeye Trail from Meigs County to Lawrence County, a distance of 48 miles, age 77

1966: Wichita, Kansas television interview

1968 1 March: Perry Clayton Gatewood died at Holzer Hospital, Gallipolis, Gallia Co., Ohio

1969: Emma received an award from Governor James

Rhodes, Ohio, for aiding conservation

1969: Emma received a trophy and a plaque from Chamber of Commerce, Gallipolis

1969: Emma received award for slogan submitted in the "Litterbug" state contest

1969 12 September: article in the *Ohio Bell/Perspective* magazine: "A Touch of Sassafras." Three sons, Monroe, Robert and Nelson, worked for Ohio Bell

1969 September: article in *The Wonderful World of Ohio* magazine about the Buckeye Trail has a photo and mentions her.

1969: Emma was made an honorary lifetime member and given the title "Director Emeritus" of the Board of Directors of the Buckeye Trail Association

1970: Scrapbooks of Emma's travels were placed in the Gallia County Library and the Ohioana Library.

1973 29 May: Ginger Kay Gilliam was born to James R. and Karen Tabor Gilliam, Monroe's great-granddaughter. Grandma's first great-great-grandchild

1973 June: Grandma Gatewood visited her first great-great-grandchild at Holzer Hospital; granddaughter Eleanor Gatewood Gilliam took her.

1973 04 June: Emma Rowena Caldwell Gatewood died at Holzer Hospital, Gallipolis, Gallia Co., Ohio

1973: A resolution by Mr. Armstrong of the Ohio State Senate presented in memory of Emma Gatewood "Grandma"

1977 July 9: Dedication of the trail named for Emma "Grandma" Gatewood on the Bob Evans Farms in Rio Grande, Ohio

1977: Grandma Gatewood's first great-great-grandchild, Ginger Gilliam, Monroe's great-granddaughter, cut the ribbon dedicating trail at Bob Evans Farm

1978 19 July: death of Ernest Monroe Gatewood

1981: A plaque dedicating a trail in the Hocking Hills of Ohio, from Old Man's Cave to Ash Cave, was named "Grandma Gatewood Memorial Hiking Trail"

1993 Fall: An article of parts of her 1964 trail diaries appeared in the *Gallia County Historical Society* newsletter

1993:An article appeared in the Buckeye Trail newsletter *Trail Blazer*, Emma was also mentioned in several of their newsletters over the years

జఎఎ

BIBLIOGRAPHIC NOTES
AND INFORMATION

‽ "All Is Forgiven." *The Toledo Blade*. August 5, 1959.
(Nelson Gatewood Collection) (klh #43)

‽ Appalachian Trail Sign Portrait. 1955. A.T.
Unknown 1955: n. page. (klh #31)

‽ "A Touch of Sassafras!" *Ohio Bell/perspective*. 12
Sept. 1969. From Ohioana Library. (Good
biographical article from when she was 82.) (klh #1)

‽ "The Buckeye Trail." *Buckeye Trail Association, Inc.
with ODNR* (1968). (Description and map of section
that Emma laid out and was also named after her.)
(Marjorie L. Wood Collection) (klh #53)

‽ *Conservation Work Appreciated*. 1969. Ohioana, Our
House Museum, Gallipolis, OH. *Times-Sentinel* 19
Oct. 1969, Sunday ed.: 1. (klh #35)

‽ "Death Of Tenant Results In Murder Charge."

Unknown Newspaper. (Article on death of Hiram Johnson plus Email from Marjorie L. Wood. Perry's murder trial.) (Marjorie L. Wood Collection) (klh #65)

ॐ "Fall Colors Hike Week Enjoyed By 35 Rugged Hikers." *Fontana Village Resort News.* Spring, 1970. (Nelson Gatewood Collection) (klh #43)

ॐ "Grandma Gatewood." Hocking Hills Internet Guide. http://hockinghills.com/i_grandm.htm (Nelson Gatewood Collection) (klh #43)

ॐ "Gatewood, Emma." Interview. Personal interview. 10 July 1954. (Handwritten diary entries by Emma. Re: reading *National Geographic* article that inspired her to hike A.T. and some of her hiking notes) (Marjorie L. Wood Collection) (klh #60)

ॐ "Grandma Gatewood." *TrailBlazer.* June 1993:

Reprint of *Buckeye Trailblazer* July 1973 tribute: "Farewell, Grandma" by Robert R. Paton, Editor. (In addition, another story about her passing written some years later.) (klh #7)

◊ "Grandma Gatewood's Experiences Are Recalled." *Oregonian* [Portland] 1964. (Oregon Trail hike and several others. Scout troop hike leader. Noted probably from Ohioana Library) (klh #28)

◊ "Grandma Takes a Hike." 1956. *The Pittsburgh Press*. October 21, 1956, sec. Roto Magazine: 1. Print. (Nelson Gatewood collection) (klh #32)

◊ "Hiking Grandma Nears Her Goal." Unknown Newspaper (Oregon Hike). (Nelson Gatewood Collection) (klh #43)

◊ "More Than 35 Participate In Blazing Buckeye Trail In Area." *Journal*. Print. City and date unknown. (Patrick Hayes Collection, BTA) (klh #6)

& "Mrs. Emma Gatewood." *Sports Illustrated* 15 Aug. 1955: (Article during her 1955 trek on A.T.) (Marjorie L. Wood Collection) (klh #50)

& "Pioneer Grandmother." *Sports Illustrated* 10 Oct. 1955: 1. No author noted. (Completion of A.T. 1955 trek; Difficult obstacles of A.T.) (Marjorie L. Wood Collection) (klh #51/duplicate of klh #33 article reference)

& "Surname Registry of Gallia County." *Home Page for Gallia Co. Genealogy Soc., OGS Inc.* N.p., n.d. Web. 5 Dec. 2010. <http://galliagenealogy.org/surnames.htm>. (Gatewood: surnames and obituaries) (klh #23)

& " 'Walking Grandmother' Dead Of Heart Attack At 85." From Unknown Pittsburg Paper. (Lucy Seeds collection) (blh #5)

૨ Adamson, Richard (Rick), BT/NCT State Trail Coordinator, BTA Executive Bd., Ohio Forest Stewardship Committee, ODNR. Email correspondence Bette Lou Higgins. July 6, 2010. (Emma segment of Buckeye Trail) (klh #3)

૨ Adamson, Richard (Rick). "Grandma Gatewood." West Salem Historical Society Meeting. West Salem Historical Society. Biographical, 6 pgs, West Salem, OH. 2 March, 2010. (klh #4)

૨ Bilton, Kathy. Email correspondence Bette Lou Higgins. 11 Aug. 2010. (Shaefer controversy) (klh#14 & klh#15)

૨ Borland, Lucille. " 'The Queen Of The Forest' Visits West View After Memorable Hike." *City and Suburban Life*. September 27, 1957. (Nelson Gatewood Collection) (klh #43)

એ Creager, Ellen. "A Lazy Hikers Guide to the Appalachian Trail." *The Chronicle Telegram* [Lorain] 7 Nov. 2010, Sunday ed., sec. D Travel/Advice: 3. *Detroit Free Press* source Re: Max Patch, App. Tr., Pisgah Nat'l Forest, NC. (klh #2)

એ Cunningham, Steve. E-mail correspondence with Bette Lou Higgins, August 14, 2014. Website: West Virginia in the Civil War (http://www.wvcivilwar.com/) *(information regarding Hugh Caldwell's Civil War service)*

એ Dale, Frank T. "Mighty and Mischievous Grandma Gatewood." *Appalachian Trailway News*. July/August, 1995.

એ Dailey, Juanita Evans. Personal interview. 4 July 2011. (Emma/Doctoring) (klh #11)

એ Downing, Bob. "In Steps Of A Busy Grandma: Ohio

Trail Honors Pioneering Hiker." *Post-Gazette.com*.

Pittsburgh Post-Gazette, 23 Feb. 2010. Web. 18

Apr. 2010. <http://www.post-gazette.com/

pg/10054/1034600-37.stm>. (Duplicate of article

in *Akron Beacon Journal* see klh#5) (klh #20)

 Fellure, Cindy. Correspondence with Bette Lou

Higgins & Rosemary Kubera Goodburn. Court of

Common Please, Gallia County, Ohio, Gallipolis,

Ohio. July 23, 2014.

 Fisher, Pamela & Barbara. "Take The Time." Poem

Dedicated To Grandma Gatewood. (Nelson

Gatewood Collection) (klh #43)

 Gambino, Megan. "History, Travel, Arts, Science,

People, Places | Smithsonian Magazine." *History,

Travel, Arts, Science, People, Places | Smithsonian

Magazine*. Smithsonian Magazine, 14 July 2009.

Web. 10 Sept. 2010. <http://
www.smithsonian.com>. "Tales from the
Appalachian Trail" (klh #18)

& Gatewood, Nelson. Collection of articles about his
mother, Emma, and family, sent to Bette Lou
Higgins 2011 - 2012. (klh #43)

& Gatewood, Nelson. "Grandma Gatewood, My
Mom." Letter to Bette Lou Higgins. March 27,
2011. (klh #43)

& Gilfillan, Merrill C. "Armed with Determination."
The Columbus Dispatch. 1 Nov. 1964, Sunday ed.,
sec. Magazine: 14, (Emma 77 years old, 3rd A.T.
hike) (noted probably from Ohioana Library) (klh
#8)

& Goodburn, Rosemary Kubera. Email correspondence
Bette Lou Higgins. 2 Sept. 2010. Bibliography of

Newspaper Articles' Excerpts from Ohioana Library, Gatewood Scrapbook (klh #34)

ꝗ Goodburn, Rosemary Kubera. Email correspondence Bette Lou Higgins. 19 Nov. 2010. (re: article from Gallipolis *Daily Tribune* 10-31-1955) (klh #24)

ꝗ Haaland, Gwen D. Feldman. "A Tribute to Trail Pioneer 'Grandma' Emma Gatewood 1887-1973." The Web Poetry Corner: Gwen D. Feldman Haaland: *www.dreamagic.com*. N.p., n.d. Web. 29 Sept. 2010. <https://tinyurl.com/Gwen-D-Feldman-Haaland >. (Poet is from Ashford, CT.) (klh #22)

ꝗ Harnden, Philip. *Journeys Of Simplicity: Traveling Light With Thomas Merton, Basho, Edward Abbey, Annie Dillard & Others*. Woodstock, VT: SkyLight Paths Pub., 2003. (List of items in duffel bag "Emma 'Grandma' Gatewood," American hiker extraordinaire) (klh #19)

🔏 Higgins, Bette Lou. Gatewood, Nelson Lewis. Phone interview. 9 Feb. 2011. (Emma's son, Lucy Seeds' brother) (klh #44)

🔏 Higgins, Bette Lou. Sullivan, Lillian Gatewood. Phone interview. 14 Oct. 2010. (Emma's granddaughter, Nelson Gatewood's daughter) (klh #42)

🔏 Higgins, Bette Lou. Personal Interview with Lillian Gatewood Sullivan. 21 Aug. 2011. (notes and audio – CD documented) (blh #8)

🔏 Higgins, Bette Lou. Email to Kelly Boyer Sagert. 1 Dec. 2010. (Shaffer controversy summary from multiple sources.) (klh #12)

🔏 Higgins, Bette Lou. E-mail and personal correspondence with Jeff Patrick. Mount Rogers Outfitters, Damascus, Virginia. July – October 2013.

(Emma's shoes/Mayer Elizabeth McKee. Pictures supplied by Presley Patrick)

🔖 Higgins, Bette Lou. Sargent, Steve. Phone Interview and e-mail correspondence. 18-27 Aug. 2014.

🔖 Higgins, Bette Lou. Bell, Harold. Phone Interview. 19 Aug. 2014.

🔖 Houck, Pat. "Conservation Honors Heaped On 'Grandma'." *Unknown* 11 Nov. 1969: (No source newspaper i.d. or date except approx. from age of Grandma) (klh #26)

🔖 Jenkins, Thomas (House Representatives). "Achievements of a Heroic American Lady." *Congressional Record-House* June 25 (1956): 1. (National Fame of Emma. Relative of Emma: O.O. McIntyre, famed NY columnist. Heroine status.)

(noted probably from Ohioana Library) (klh #30/klh #61)

& Linkletter, Art. Interview by Art Linkletter. Phone interview. 5 Aug. 1959. (Telegram inviting Emma to be on the Art Linkletter television show on Monday, Aug, 10, 1959.) (Marjorie L. Wood Collection) (klh #59

& Marsh, W.W. *Oregon Centennial Expo* 4 Apr. 1959: 30. (From the Marjorie L. Wood collection Documents (4): Two Oregon Centennial News Releases; Two Receipts of her clothing as memorabilia for the Oregon Historical Society) (klh #58)

& Marshall, Louise B. "Grandma Gatewood (1887-1973).*Unknown Magazine*. (Nelson Gatewood Collection) (klh #43)

℣ McCoy, Eva R. "Meet Mrs. Gatewood – The Hiker And The Person." *Gallipolis Daily Tribune* 31 Oct. 1955, sec. Features Women Fancy: (First A.T. hike 1955) (klh#25)

℣ Montgomery, Ben. Grandma Gatewood's Walk. Chicago Review Press. Chicago, 2014.

℣ Montgomery, Ben. Interview with Bette Lou Higgins. 1 August 2014.

℣ Ohio Department of Vital Statistics. Columbus, Ohio.

℣ Paton, Robert R., Editor "Farewell, Grandma." *Buckeye Trailblazer.* Volume 6, No. 3. July 1973: Columbus, Ohio. (Original tribute article regarding her death) (klh #9)

℣ Patton, Linda. Email correspondence Bette Lou Higgins. 10 Aug. 2010. (Mildred Lamb: 1st female

thru hiker – with companion. Clarification Emma
1st female solo hiker of entire A.T.) (klh #21)

🍂 Potteiger, Laurie. Email correspondence Bette Lou
Higgins. 1 Nov. 2011. (A.T. mileage) (blh #111)

🍂 Seeds, Lucy. Personal interview. 30 June 2009.
(Emma as described by youngest daughter, Lucy
Seeds) (klh #36)

🍂 Seeds, Lucy. Personal interview and collection of
memorabilia. 18 Nov. 2010. (klh #40)

🍂 Seeds, Lucy. Email correspondence Bette Lou
Higgins. 7 Jan. 2011. (Emma's children's names.)
(klh #37)

🍂 Seeds, Lucy. Email correspondence Bette Lou
Higgins. 23 Feb. 2011. (Stories of memories of
Emma.) (klh #38)

🍂 Seeds, Lucy. Email correspondence Bette Lou

Higgins. 11 June 2011. (Snakes and newspaper man stories.) (klh #39)

ʚ Seeds, Lucy. Blessing School picture (from her collection). Sent 31 August 2011. (blh #4)

ʚ Seeds, Lucy. Correspondence with Bette Lou Higgins. (Timeline of hike and diary entries from 1966.) (blh #6)

ʚ Seeds, Lucy. Email correspondence Bette Lou Higgins. 14 September 2011. (Diary and question: height & weight.) (blh #1)

ʚ Seeds, Lucy. Email correspondence Bette Lou Higgins. (Miscellaneous correspondence during the entire project.) (blh #1)

ʚ Shaffer, John. Email correspondence Bette Lou Higgins. 11 Aug. 2010. (Controversy issue discussion with Earl Shaffer's brother.) (klh #13)

❧ Sowash, Rick. "The Galloping Grandma." *Ohio LTAP Quarterly* 24.3 (2008): 7. Excerpts under "Extraordinary Ohioans" taken from Chapter 19 of Heroes of Ohio: *23 True Tales of Courage and Character* (1998) Book available from www.sowash.com (klh #17)

❧ Sullivan, Ann. "Hostess House." *The Oregonian* [Portland] 8 Aug. 1959, Saturday ed., sec. Three: 1-4. (Oregon Trail hike of Emma.) (noted probably from Ohioana Library) (klh #29)

❧ Sullivan, Lillian Gatewood and Pagyn Alexander. Grandma Gatewood Walks Across America. Limited ed. Dayton, Ohio (P.O. Box 96-A, Dayton 45449-2045): Pine Needle Press, 1993. (klh #41)

❧ Townsend, Irene. "Son Of Hiking Granny Tells Of Her Experience." Unknown Newspaper. Eastmont,

Newcom North. (Nelson Gatewood Collection) (klh #43)

  Urbine, Joel P. Email correspondence Bette Lou Higgins. 12 Aug. 2010. (Shaffer controversy.) (klh #16)

  Walker, Nancy. Collection of e-mail correspondence and related documents/news articles/poems sent to Bette Lou Higgins. Recollections of her Grandmother Carrie Elam – cousin to Emma Gatewood. 2012.

  Wikipedia. Oregon Trail Map from 1907; Public Domain Image, http://en.wikipedia.org/wiki/ Oregon_Trail

  Wood, Marjorie L. Email correspondence Bette Lou Higgins. 14 Mar. 2011. (Great granddaughter, description of Emma.) (klh #10)

> Wood, Marjorie L. Personal interview with Bette Lou Higgins & Peter Huston. 16 Apr. 2011. (The Caldwell family listing, Emma's parents and siblings.) (Marjorie L. Wood Collection) (klh #55)

> Wood, Marjorie L. Personal interview. 16 Apr. 2011 with Bette Lou Higgins & Peter Huston. (Collection 3 poems by Emma. "That Elusive Bug" won the Conservation Contest from the State of Ohio.) (Marjorie L. Wood Collection) (klh #54)

> Wood, Marjorie L. Personal interview. 16 Apr. 2011 with Bette Lou Higgins & Peter Huston. (Emma's home remedies.) (Marjorie L. Wood Collection) (klh #49)

> Wood, Marjorie L. Personal interview. 16 Apr. 2011 with Bette Lou Higgins & Peter Huston. (Hiking record of Emma. List of honors. Death Certificate copy.) (Marjorie L. Wood Collection) (klh #56)

Wood, Marjorie L. Personal interview. 16 Apr. 2011 with Bette Lou Higgins & Peter Huston. (Trip to Gallipolis, Ohio photographs of family members, Crown City house and barn, artifacts, Emma as a child, her gravesite, diaries, and hiking beret.) (Marjorie L. Wood Collection) (klh #48)

Wood, Marjorie L. Personal interview. 16 Apr. 2011 with Bette Lou Higgins & Peter Huston. (Assorted writings and one recipe by Emma) (Marjorie L. Wood Collection) (klh #57)

Wood, Marjorie L. Personal interview. 16 Apr. 2011 with Bette Lou Higgins & Peter Huston. (Uncle Robert, WWII, prisoner of war) (Marjorie L. Wood Collection) (klh #62)

Wood, Marjorie L. Personal interview. 16 Apr. 2011

with Bette Lou Higgins & Peter Huston. (Uncle Robert, WWII, MIA) (Marjorie L. Wood Collection) (klh #63)

& Wood, Marjorie L. Personal interview. 16 Apr. 2011 with Bette Lou Higgins & Peter Huston. (Two photos of Emma's mother at home in CA) (Marjorie L. Wood Collection) (klh #64)

& Wood, Marjorie L. Personal interview. 16 Apr. 2011 with Bette Lou Higgins & Peter Huston. (Photo of shoes.) (klh #66)

& Wood, Marjorie L. Personal interview. 16 Apr. 2011 with Bette Lou Higgins & Peter Huston. (Notes from Emma's diary 1955, 1959, 1918) (Marjorie L. Wood Collection) (klh #47)

& Wood, Marjorie L. Personal interview. 16 Apr. 2011 with Bette Lou Higgins & Peter Huston. "Interview with Marjorie Lynn Wood and Bette Lou Higgins" (Biographical-Emma lineage, husband Perry's lineage) (Marjorie L. Wood Collection) (klh #46)

ɮ Wood, Marjorie L. Personal interview. 16 Apr. 2011 with Bette Lou Higgins & Peter Huston. ("Grandma Emma Caldwell Gatewood's Appalachian Trail Diary." 1955 "Emma Gatewood's First Appalachian Trail Trip" Diary excerpts 1954.) (Marjorie L. Wood Collection) (klh #52)

ɮ Wood, Marjorie L. Email correspondence Bette Lou Higgins. 21 July 2011. Personal correspondence with Bette Lou Higgins. (Perry Gatewood, Emma's husband) (klh #45)

ɮ Wood, Marjorie L. Email correspondence Bette Lou Higgins. August 16, 2011. Timeline. (blh #3)

ଏ Wood, Marjorie L. Email correspondence Bette Lou Higgins. September 2, 2011. (Death Date.) (blh #2)

ଏ Wood, Marjorie L. Email correspondence Bette Lou Higgins. October 4, 2011. (Abuse/Marjorie/Lucy) (blh #7)

ଏ Wood, Marjorie L. Email correspondence Bette Lou Higgins. Miscellaneous correspondence during the entire project. (blh #2)

ଏ Unknown Personal interview. 1969. Anon notes-- Hiking Record of Emma 1955-1969.(klh #27)

ଏଏଏ

E:\gatewood\scripts\book version\kindleprint\gatewoodamazonv2.pub r060418

Eden Valley

From **Canal Songs and Stories**, a fun and informative program that features music and stories from the Ohio-Erie Canal, to **Doctor Putnam's Miracle Mixture**, a vivid, high-spirited living history program, Eden Valley gives your audiences drama that brims with energy, humor, and fantasy and features a magical cast of characters.

Eden Valley has written and/or produced theatrical programs for many of Northern Ohio's most prestigious educational and cultural organizations including:

*The Cleveland Metroparks
*The Steamship *William G. Mather*
*The Great Lakes Historical Society
*The Western Reserve Historical Society
*The Cleveland Health Education Museum

Programs include:
Cleveland Sings!
Lady Of The Lake
Ohio Ghost Stories
From Ohio To Broadway
Stories From A Christmas Past
You Can't Play Ball In A Skirt!
Tales From The Western Reserve
Trail Magic: The Grandma Gatewood Story

Eden Valley Enterprises is dedicated to providing unique educational experiences. Our philosophy is that learning and doing are fun and our basic tool is theatre. Through living history programs, storytelling performances, and musical trips back in time, EVE provides an entertaining and educational opportunity for all ages.

Dedicated to the expansion of horizons through the arts, sciences and humanities, Eden Valley is a springboard from which people can enjoy the world with a little bit more understanding and joy.

OHIO GHOST STORIES is the companion book to Eden Valley's storytelling program of the same name. It is just one of EVE's history programs which cover topics such as **REMARKABLE OHIOANS** and **ORDINARY PEOPLE IN EXTRAORDINARY TIMES: STORIES FROM WWII** — many of which have companion books.

Eden Valley has a wide assortment of existing programs available for presentation and if these programs don't meet your needs, we'd be happy to put together one especially for you! If you would like to arrange a performance for your group or would like more information about any of Eden Valley services, programs and publications, e-mail us at blheve@edenvalleyenterprises.org or visit our website at www.edenvalleyenterprises.org.

EDEN VALLEY

1250 East River St.
Elyria, Ohio 44035

E-mail: blheve@edenvalleyenterprises.org
www.edenvalleyenterprises.org